Why Am I A Christian?

And More Questions To Examine Your Faith

Ryan Johnson • Zac Johnson

Penitent Press

Dedicated to those courageous

enough to ask questions

Introduction

"True wisdom comes to each of us when we realize how little we understand about life, ourselves, and the world around us."

Socrates

As humans we are born with the innate ability to learn. We learn to walk and talk. For the first few years of our lives we are constantly learning every day. We irritate our parents with our continuous questioning. But with the onset of adolescence and adulthood we begin to believe we have most things figured out. We learn our trade and develop opinions on politics and religion, we stop asking questions and as a result we stop learning. There are many factors involved in this change. As children we have not yet acquired the sense of infallibility that we develop as we grow older. As children we ask questions with no sense of embarrassment. We don't worry about sounding foolish or being called stupid. We have no fear of being wrong.

As children we live in a world of uncertainty, and we spend all of our time attempting to figure things out. We begin to form opinions about the world in an effort to take control over our lives. But as we develop dogmatic opinions and beliefs and cling to our assumptions, we rarely question the evidence our beliefs are based on. As human beings we often seem terrified of learning new things and discovering new truths and so time and again we choose the security and comfort of the status quo, afraid of the unfamiliarity of change.

We come to you as men. Men who are ever aware of our own fallibility. Who know all too well how to make mistakes. Who are far from perfect and frequently wrong. We offer this book as a window into our lives. This book of questions traces our own journey. We want every reader to know that these questions were first asked to ourselves and then to each other and now we share them with you and hope they are found to be helpful. Perhaps you have just begun to ask yourself some of these important questions, if so our prayers are with you and we are thankful for your courage. Perhaps you have been on this search for awhile and know the feeling of confusion well. We share in your feelings and experiences as you question yourselves and then struggle to find the courage to share your feelings and your questions with those around you.

These questions are meant for introspection, not just to instigate arguments with others who may have differing opinions. This is by no means a complete list of all useful questions. This is merely a starting point for learning and serious thinking. We are very interested in questions that come to the minds of our readers as well. We have included an email address below where you can send us questions, and we are very appreciate of you and your thoughts. May we all grow together in grace and knowledge.

Contact us at penitentpress@live.com

1

Why am I a Christian?

2

Do I only pray when something is going wrong in my life?

3

Is God my hope for reconciling my sin or my excuse to sin?

4

If someone held a gun to my head and told me all I had to do to live was deny Jesus being my lord and savior what would I do?

5

Do I mold God into what I want him to be, or do I accept him for whom and what he is?

6

Am I willing to die for my beliefs?

7

Would I be willing to die for a stranger?

8

If a complete stranger observed me for a week, would they be able to determine that I am a Christian?

9

If love is only a feeling, how do others know I love them?

10

Do I compare myself to people around me or to Jesus?

11

Do I honestly seek the truth?
Or do I stop once I've found
something I agree with?

12

Do I consider myself a citizen of the kingdom of God or America?

13

Do I act in the same manner both in and out of church?

14

Is there a difference between faith and belief? If so what is it?

15

Do I study the Bible for myself or do I rely solely on my pastors opinions?

16

Does God care what clothes I wear to church?

17

Do I avoid non-Christians, and if so why?

18

Do I put more time and effort into my career or in furthering God's kingdom?

19

Am I willing to question my faith? If not then can I be 100% confident that every aspect of it is correct?

20

33% of the world's population identify themselves as Christians. Why don't we have a bigger impact?

21

Am I a Christian? Disciples were first called Christians because they were like Christ. Am I Christ-like?

22

Do I share the same beliefs as my parents? If so have I ever questioned those beliefs?

23

Have I read from the Bible recently, and if not why not?

24

Do I know all of the Ten Commandments?

25

Jesus died for all humanity, even murderers. Would I sacrifice myself to save a murderer?

26

Am I a different person since becoming a Christian? Would my friends and family agree with me?

27

If I found my family murdered and the killer got away but returned in a year to ask for my forgiveness, could I forgive him?

28

Am I afraid of dying?

29

Do I pay attention in church?

30

Are church buildings necessary?

31

Is the "American dream" compatible with Christianity?

32

If I am to love my enemies,
is war ever justified?

33

Would I be willing to kill for
my country?

34

Christians are rarely persecuted in America, if that changed would I continue to practice my faith?

35

Is punishment a requirement for justice?

36

Is peace only a goal or the means by which we reach that goal?

37

What is the kingdom of God?

38

What is the kingdom of heaven?

39

Where is the kingdom of heaven?

40

Are the kingdom of heaven and the kingdom of God the same thing?

41

Is Christ Jesus' last name?

42

Is faith mere belief or something more?

43

What is the significance of
the phrase "Son of Man"?

44

What is the significance of
the phrase "Son of God"?

45

What does amen mean? If I don't know why do I say it at the end of every prayer?

46

What is a disciple? Am I a disciple?

47

What is an apostle?

48

What does it mean to repent? Is it only an admission of guilt?

49

Should Christians be afraid of God?

50

What will heaven be like?
Where did my ideas of
heaven come from?

51

What will hell be like?
Where did my ideas of hell
come from?

52

Does going to church
constitute following Jesus?

53

Was Jesus' only purpose to
save me from my sins?

54

Are all of the books of the Bible of equal importance?

55

Should the Bible be read differently than any other book?

56

Is the flesh evil? Should I hope to escape from it?

57

As a Christian, should I speak out against evil?

58

Did Jesus promise Christians success and prosperity?

59

Is Adam responsible for my sins?

60

Did Jesus come to give us rules to live by or to free us from the burden of rules?

61

Should any other written works be studied in addition to the Bible? If not, why not?

62

What led me to become a
Christian?

63

What is a Christian?

64

Is it right for Christians to separate themselves or their families from the world?

65

What did Jesus mean when he said his kingdom was not of this world?

66

Once I've become a Christian, is my mission on earth finished?

67

Should Christians be active in politics?

68

Do I spend more time defending my faith than living it?

69

Is my focus on getting to heaven or bringing God's kingdom to earth?

70

Do I praise God in the bad times as well as the good?

71

Do I have a dualistic worldview? If so why?

72

Is my congregations focus on building up the congregation or bringing people to Christ? Is there a difference?

73

Should we baptize our children before they are old enough to make the decision on their own?

74

If there were discrepancies between two biblical accounts would that discredit the Bible?

75

Do pastors have any special authority over other Christians?

76

Am I confident in the accuracy of my particular Bible translation?

77

Do I know the history of how the Bible came to be?

78

Is it okay for Christians to be upset after being wronged as long as they eventually forgive, or should forgiveness precede transgression?

79

God gave people dominion over the earth trusting us to look after it, how are we doing?

80

Why did Jesus ask so many questions?

81

Why do I believe what I believe?

82

Is the Bible hard for me to understand? If so why do I think God would make it so complicated?

83

Is context important when reading the Bible or do the words transcend time and culture?

84

If the books of the New Testament were written after Jesus ascended to heaven then anytime he mentions the scriptures must he have been referring to The Old Testament? If so does this make me reconsider the importance of The Old Testament?

85

Have I ever read the any of the books of the Bible all the way through from start to finish?

86

How do I know the Bible is true?

87

What is the Word of God?

88

What is the mission of the church?

89

What is the hope of disciples of Jesus?

90

If I have absolutely no idea
what huge texts of scripture
are about, do I think I am
informed enough to make
sweeping judgments?

91

Why were Jesus' followers
persecuted?

92

Why was Jesus crucified?

93

Do I find it strange that Jesus never said "here's how you go to heaven" or something similar?

94

What is God's revelation to man?

95

Why did God create humans?

96

Do I truly believe in God or do I just do it because it's popular?

97

If Jesus came up to me and said "leave your job, house and family and give everything you own to the poor, and be ready to die" would I go?

98

If a stranger was on the side of the road would I bring him to my house, feed him and give him a place to sleep?

99

Do I only reach out to people who have similar beliefs?

100

If someone asked me today how to be saved could I tell them?

101

If I think I would help someone if they knocked on my door and asked for help, what's the difference between that person and someone 1000 miles away, 100, 10?

102

Do I keep some commandments but not others? Do I visit prisoners or support widows?

103

Have I ever honestly made the decision to devote my life to following Jesus?

104

Jesus said to love your enemies, who is left to hate?

105

Do I consider myself a good Christian?

106

Are the oils mentioned in the Bible still useful today?

107

Do I consider context when studying the bible?

108

Are my prayers primarily centered on myself? Do I pray enough for others?

109

Can I know Jesus like his
apostles did?

110

What would the world look
like if everyone were like me?

111

What is the work of the
Holy Spirit?

112

What is the significance of
baptism?

113

How should the Jesus community view/treat animals and the earth?

114

How does Jesus' command to not resist evil apply in the world today on the individual, community and world levels?

115

Does patriotism conflict
with the command to love
your enemies?

116

Is the God of the Old Testament the same God of the New Testament?

117

What should the attitude
and actions of Jesus
followers be toward Muslims?

118

Can I be certain that Adam and Eve were real people? Does it matter?

119

How is God's original creation different from the world today?

120

Do I feel I have to make time in my life for Jesus or is Jesus my life?

121

If my reason for being a Christian is a feeling, how can I argue with someone of another religion who uses the same argument?

122

Can I define God?

123

Can I define holiness?

124

Is my definition of God compatible with the God of the Bible?

125

Do the people who reject Christianity do so because they've studied the Bible and don't believe it or because of the reputation of Christians?

126

Am I so sure of my beliefs that I don't need to study the Bible?

127

Why are there so many different denominations in Christianity? Is this a bad thing?

128

Is it possible to be beyond
forgiveness?

129

What does it mean to be
born again?

130

Do I feel as comfortable at church as I do at my job?

131

Should I argue over the merits of Christianity with non-Christians?

132

Why did the majority of Jews
reject Jesus as the messiah?

133

How does the Bible define
the trinity?

134

Will everyone be equal in heaven?

135

Jesus said to love your neighbor as yourself, who is my neighbor?

136

If Christianity or any aspect of it were made illegal how would I respond? Would it prevent me from being a witness of Jesus?

137

What does it mean that Jesus has all authority in heaven and on earth?

138

Are the Ten Commandments the only commands that we are to follow?

139

Why do we celebrate Christmas? When and how did that tradition start?

140

How does Jesus say we can distinguish between a true Christian and a lukewarm Christian?

141

Is idolatry only a problem of the past or something that we still struggle with today?

142

What does Jesus mean when he says "your will be done on earth as it is in heaven" while reciting the Lord's Prayer?

143

How did Christianity go from a radical unpopular movement to the largest religion in the world? Is modern Christianity the same as it was in the first century?

144

What does the term "Bible" mean?

145

Do I take the genre into account when I read the books of the Bible?

146

What is the importance of prayer? Are we to position ourselves in a certain way when we pray?

147

What was the purpose for all the rules and regulations the Jews had to follow?

148

Do I personally know
Jesus?

149

Do women and men enjoy
equal freedom in Christ?

150

Should Christians avoid alcohol, gambling and tattoos and if so, why?

151

Is there any way I can make my life a little more like heaven?

152

Why does God rely so much on us humans to spread his message?

153

How do I demonstrate my faith on a daily basis?

154

What do I actually stand for?

155

If I won millions of dollars in the lottery, would it change me?

156

Would I still trust and believe in God if I lost everything?

157

What does it mean for my life if Jesus really did return from the dead?

158

How willing am I to
question my own beliefs?

159

Is it possible that my beliefs
are wrong?

160

Is there sufficient evidence to come to warrant my beliefs? What assumptions, if any, are my conclusions based on?

161

Do I use the scriptures to justify already held beliefs or to positively change how I think and act?

162

Do I have the grace to let other people be wrong?

163

Do I live a lifestyle of reconciliation?

164

Is the redeeming love of God evident in the way I talk and communicate with people?

165

How do my decisions of what I eat, wear, purchase etc. affect the rest of humanity and creation?

166

Do I define myself by the things I'm against?

167

Do I blame God when something doesn't go my way?

168

Does the way I talk perpetuate love or violence, hate and exclusion?

169

How many times do I have to forgive my brother?

170

Am I a good listener?

171

Do I love myself?

172

Am I quick to call the beliefs of others into question but not to question my own beliefs?

173

Is death God's will?

174

Where is God when I hurt?
What is he doing?

175

What does it mean to be
made in God's image?

176

What does it mean to be
truly human?

177

Why did God create man?

178

What is the meaning of life?

179

In what ways does my culture/society influence the way I see the world?

180

Do I view other people through the lens, prejudices, biases of my culture and experiences?

181

Do I read scripture always investigating its context or do I force my 21st century American context on the text?

182

Does the overall direction of my life reveal an evident growth in knowledge and grace?

183

Am I constantly learning?

184

In what ways does truth set us free?

186

Are my opinions developing by continual learning or have they remained stagnant for a prolonged period?

187

Do I see every person I come in contact with and every situation in life as a learning opportunity?

188

Do I love all people or just my close group of family and friends?

189

When I reach the end of my life, will I wonder what I missed?

190

Should Christians act as God's police in the world, enforcing his laws and commands?

191

Do the other elements of creation (land, plants, animals etc.) exist merely for our consumption or did God have other intentions when creating them?

192

Who is more Christ-like, someone who is affiliated with a Christian Church but whose life is devoid of service, love, justice and peace or one who is unaffiliated with any Church but actively serves his fellow man?

193

Will the effects of your actions have to be corrected by God when the world is renewed or do they build upon Gods Kingdom leaving less for him to do?

194

How is the kingdom of God different from the kingdoms of the world?

195

What is the Tree of the
Knowledge of Good and Evil?

196

What forms of idolatry are
practiced in my culture?

197

The command to not be afraid is the most used command in the Bible? Does that surprise you?

198

What is wisdom?

199

What is the gospel?

200

Will there be animals in heaven?

201

Why did Jesus speak using parables?

202

If heaven is the perfect world that God intended to create why are we living in this corrupted world?

203

If everyone is my neighbor, should I help those in need even if they live in another state, or even another country?

204

When God created the world, did he include everything man needs for good health? If not, what was lacking?

205

Can I rightly call myself pro-life if I support war and capital punishment?

206

Does God give arbitrary commands?

207

Do I know everything?

208

Do I know everything that
is important?

209

If I don't know everything
how do I know that I know
everything that is important?

www.ingramcontent.com/pod-product-compliance
Lightning Source LLC
Chambersburg PA
CBHW021153020426
42331CB00003B/38